Jake Berry

Trilogy:Kenosis

Lavender Ink
lavenderink.org

Trilogy:Kenosis
Jake Berry

Copyright © 2018 by the author and Diálogos Books.

All rights reserved. No part of this work may be reproduced
in any form without the express written permission
of the copyright holders and Diálogos Books.

Printed in the U.S.A.
First Printing
10 9 8 7 6 5 4 3 2 1   18 19 20 21 22 23

Book design: Bill Lavender
Front cover image by Jake Berry.

Library of Congress Control Number 2018961913:
Berry, Jake
Trilogy:Kenosis / Jake Berry;
p. cm.
ISBN: 978-1-944884-55-0 (pbk.)

Lavender Ink
lavenderink.org

An earlier version of "Scale" appeared in E•ratio

TRILOGY:KENOSIS

Sheila E. Murphy, Neeli Cherkovski, Ivan Argüelles, Willie Smith, Jack Foley, Jeffrey Side, Jack Random

TRILOGY:KENOSIS

SCALE

for Gregory Vincent St. Thomasino

1

If we have been in that house
    it is no longer a house
    but a field

charged
resonant

mound
& stone

after Beth-el
a dream like lightning

unkempt in all his ways

These are the vestments
Triune
Polyphonic

a cradle
made of voices

a cradle
before the interruption
(before the incision)
of glass

2

If it begins
it begins
in a wound

& graceless stumbling

across a bed of silence

grotesque
until she comes into focus

3

everything crucified
and torn apart

      of sudden, terrible beauty
      a crimson light

is an occasion
to rejoice

4

out from – sheltering
as the lungs
across the bed
toward zero   (face to face)

This is our habitation

to visit
along the way

dust on our
        rags

5

[discovered]
a femur
a pelvis

a shoulder blade

    upon which
    inscribed in Greek
    (as was the Orphic inclination):

    body   σῶμα   soma
    water   ὕδωρ   hudor
    spirit   πνεῦμα pneuma

an octave apart

a spike in the earth

6

of number
there is only

a chasm

of every form
emptying

7

The word
has shaken us
free

with an essential,
forbidden
summoning

more than knowledge
more than life

a music
one step beyond

A Second Octave

1

At first
returning

The point
A scarlet veil
over a blue-yellow
      sun

Was that
  a rush of water?
  A fluttering?
 that took you?

Whether in or outside
I don't know

only

the opening
expanse

2

Easter
for Jack Foley

Out of death –
  such abundant nothingness –
  a fire is lit
  in the imagination

  (who understands this mysterious capacity?)

Even the seeds we do not want
spring to life

We wept
when he was taken from us
even though we did not know
who or what he was

All those dead
taken away
But our sorrow
cannot prevent spring arriving

The dead seed blooms
Our eyes itch and tear
    We struggle for breath

From disappearance
appearance is rejuvenated

We rush
to the feast
We devour fresh life
out of the dead body

We still do not know
who he was

or who set the feast

We only know
we are hungry

and only spring
can save us

3

Ice in the bed
    Weeds in the ice
The mattress returned
    to ground
    for a blood letting
behind the fences
The fathers shoved them around
    fat and ripe
    to pay for the stench
to draw out the water
    30 feet down
below where the ice can reach
    and the fire birds swam

4

Elements they called them
    Each with a name and number
    to dispel chaos
For this they chose her face
    and painted her hands
crimson black
and called for the elements
    as if they would answer
    any random signal
(had nothing to do with them)

5

When the ice rose
    & weeds took the bedding
we heard music
    out of the old elm
where only hives were known
    & those full of poison
(this before the mind caught fire)
It was only summer
    But it had never been
and her hands were clean
    and her face disappeared

6

When the click of insomnia
    loaded the rifle
and the day ignited
the dog knows his master
    when he eats him
Even the pavement
    is alive and fertile
I carry you across
and you vanish into the feathers
    of the bed grandmother spread
and we fell asleep
    with the old clock tolling
    through the wet summer streets,
    and our open window
& the odor of rain
    carried us across

Memory is more
    than what we remember and imagine –
    It is the past made sacred

7

for David Thomas Roberts

Bring on the scarlet
   in the shepherd's house
There's blood in the wool
   and blood in the hinges
   on the old screen door

   singing a hymn
   the Anatolians wove
   from a vulture's cry

   and the pregnant queen
   tore a brooding god
   from the leopard's throat

   where flesh
   is so thin and tender
   it vibrates in every microtone
   the deep soul mourns

   There were men in the field
speaking to the limestone
   the language of a stellar sea

   of regions in the sky long forgotten
   before the scribes took hold
   and the code was frozen

   how a man might

stake his being in the land
& women became property

But in the dark corners
of a ramshackle town
we conspire an infinity
We recreate the name
the landlord gave us
to cast across the generations

to forget the torture
the sheer hell
of coming awake

in the terrible cloister
of the body
behind fearful, righteous eyes

Bring on the scarlet
and plant fossilized teeth
in a cocoon of nebulae

waiting for the resurrection
a million years ago
and waiting still

Bring on the scarlet
a syringe of rain
sewn beneath the skin
a filigree of veins
where the sky begins

Kenosis

Heaven is empty.
Nothing but blue forever.

Weather in the wires
  three weeks old.

The signal breaks down,
fragments of fragments
vanishing into the raw pulse of static

    No self at all,
    so the mechanists would have it
    & the ascetics as well,
    finding no trace in their bones
    & no place to keep it

So love is merely
an eloquent triune descent
into the dead fact of matter

    Can you feel gravel
    where the sky used to be?

    to wear death
    like a glory shroud
    because it is all that remains of truth?

Here is knowledge
bifurcated and splayed upon a tree
The feast has seized us

down in our joints
and inscribed her gray miracle
for the last thing
for those that thrive on last things
for the animal mirror
afraid to look you in the face

In the pleroma of nothingness
all knowledge is revealed as fakery
    as sublime ornament
    as gorgeous foolishness

We are bound by the kisses we drink

If I stumble walking toward you
it's not because I'm drunk
I am blinded by neon geometries
that exist nowhere
not even in my eyes

With total absence of Being
With oblivion as my lover
With love for her and none other
disappear

        Even death wears out its use,
        surrenders and dies
        as all creations must

        Brooding
        through the twilight of late autumn

Brooding
over the waters
where Chaos sleeps
Brooding
in these dead streets
a sullen old man
while the years slip away

Heaven is surely empty

Do you know the violence in a name?

She brought me
a ring and a cross on a necklace
and a long wool coat
She brought me
the eyes of a dozen strangers
She brought me a kiss
worth dying for

Now the days come like electric shocks
Every moment is a separate particle
in another orbit

The body is a shell
hollowed by wind and water,
merciless heat and bitter cold
and a lifetime of desire

But the body is where light begins

The books have been swept clean of
of words and images
The pages come to life

God, I am with you
in no man's land

    For he who could not discover
    the foundations of the house
    For she who struggled
    in the abyss of the Trinity
    For he who fought hand to hand
    with a legion of belligerent angels
    For she who wept when the tree
    exploded in flames
    For he who drowned in her tears
    For she who buried him,
    summoned his breath and
    with a kiss brought him back

Heaven is empty
and emptiness is a call

    Is the desire for absence
    the absence of desire?

"I have become a question to my self," St. Augustine said.
I have thrown the self into question
into judgement
into that blissful moment when

consciousness slips away from self
into the vast expanse of sleep

$$3 = 1 = 0$$

I felt as if I was falling apart
My hands were in motion
but they weren't my own
My eyes caught the light
and studied the world
but I was not the one seeing

You must enter the house
without entering it
As something less than a ghost
Leave no trace on the floor
no sign in the room
of your passing

Silence is the beginning of prayer
and its constant substance

(In the painting
she is weary,
her face resting on her right hand
while from her drooping left land
her ring slips
and falls onto her prayer book
The skeletal memento mori
peering over her shoulder

with his accomplice, a cherubim with a poison dart)

All those who seek the mysteries
learn the "darkness of God"

Hope is born in desolation and waste
Hope is born of despair
There is nothing else left to do

> The man swinging from the gallows
> has lost everything
> > except nothing

And so it begins
in a shining breath
in the middle of nowhere
(which cannot have a center)

> Who is sleeping under the arch?
> Who can substantiate our faith?
> How did everything we remember never happen?

Heaven is empty
Emptiness is form

> The sanctuary was so quiet
> we heard the bread when she tore it

> Love demands a beloved

When the bees were all that remained

of the ancient living things
they clawed at her back
until they tore off her wings

From out of that wound
seven rivers flowed
When she reached to fly she wept
When she wept the rivers flooded

And though the bees had devoured her
out of honest hunger
they were sorrowful
and brought her pollen
from the Void beyond worlding

From the pollen she made shapes
and poured the life of her flight into them

She set them free
in the lush green valleys
the flooded rivers created

And every first day
the garbagemen take them away
not knowing what to do with
truck loads of living creatures

From this science
a tale depends
in a single shinning breath

in the middle of nowhere
in the sticks and brambles
a fire
where lightning struck

     Aristotle uses the word 'psyche' for both
               soul and butterfly –

Out of what hellish labyrinthine earth
does the caterpillar rise
to feed and weave and die?
The rich ornaments of the tabernacle,
incense day and night,
the vestments, breastplate
and glowing stones, Urim and Thummim
Into that holy of holies
the plague worm crawls
insatiably hungry
for release from its ravenous agony
skin beneath skin
shell beneath shell
intellect and reason
handsomely adorned
in the delicate finery of a skull,
the neural arch,
the beckoning ascent
toward some oblivious absence
that renders that first, shinning breath
               essential,
               inevitable

Heaven is empty
Emptiness is form

    Call it the heart
    and lose what remains of the mind

    Plato crawls out of
    some Orphic spasm,
    a neolithic dance, a seizure
    where the animals,
    salamander, coelacanth and hawk
    ascend, carved in relief
    on the stones

Heaven is empty
Everything depends upon it

I borrowed your body
and dove into the sea
The water rose like a sky
until I had forgotten a time before water
I forgot that I drowned
and spent 7 years?
I don't know how long,
beneath the floor of the sea
where the roots of the world take form

I talked to people in cafes, tombs and streets
about what it meant
to breathe
to shine

to remember another life before drowning
I remembered your small hands
and pursed blue mouth
and I was sorry for taking your body.
Sorrow disintegrated me
and whatever remained rose.
I thought I was flying
but I was only floating to the surface
to be discovered by a child in a row boat
who fell into a fever
and wrote thousands of pages
about the body she had formed
and built a reliquary around

The pilgrimages have taken their toll
I sit still and wait for your return
to claim what is yours
to become human again
to eat and drink and laugh again
in a form only you could make
before birth
before the lie of knowledge
before the eyes lost sight
and the heart lost its voice, its gathered reckoning
and perpetual dawn flashed unrelentingly
across every wing,
every branch and face

    We have constructed an absence
    to avoid the first death
    but the first death

is all that can save us

We search for the substance
in a name,
in a voice
rising out of the river
an old forgotten god
woven into a nightmare under the low limbs

We wait for the weather to exhaust itself
before we return to the hunt

I saw you there
writing in a forbidden language
on your lover's skin
out on loan
to anyone willing to pay the price
to anyone who truly understands
the biology of sacrifice

We surrender
to the final litany
of the empirical age:
I kiss you!
I love you!
I don't want anything to do with you

unless you bring money

Even then,
even then,

just leave it by the door and disappear

In her dream she said
"These books smell like dead people."
  (roses, lilac and fermented musk)

These are priceless commodities
sold for nothing more than a glimpse
of paradise along the avenues
and riverside shops
where the fog is a language
and the rain never stops

    Who was she
    that stole my soul?
    (or was that an overcoat?)
    and tossed it into the air
    and it has yet to come down

    Let me drown again
    Let me feel the fever in the wine
    let servitude be my chosen vice

Oblivion is not forgetting
Oblivion has no mind to forget

      (Remember to die (memento mori)
        even though death has lost its power)

Oblivion is not the opposite of memory.
It is its companion and completion.

Time is no way
to measure eternity
(which has no measure).

It was said in those days,
"He is lost in heart thought."

Did you not see me
in your dark sleep
coming like fire
between the halved carcasses?

Before you existed
I surrendered to your death
and felt each cell explode
until nothing remained
but darkness and distance
and your sleeping breath
suddenly shinning

zero glittering fountain out of the well
the brutal divine come to Sumer
via the way of the animals ascending
sweet river psyche whole boundless sea
before dwarf galaxy shimmering awake
to know in some dim mirror
that I AM and trembling at the sight
brave Arjuna reduced to tears,
chrysalitic death and wet wings flashing
every altar, every stele, full of animal selves

to rediscover what the mirror knows down to dust –
From them the seraphim serpents come
Fire from the helix
Fire on the tongue
Fire in the temple and secret vaults
where gold goes to waste, rust and devilment
market charlatans who'll bring
the work of civilization down,
down to dust
from which the light took shape

Where the body ends
the river fans out across the plain
into a chorus,
a disparate harmony of the waters
rising and falling
singing a polyphonous song

Down into hell on the second day,
the crows in the morning
to clean the bones
and send the spirit home,
The geese in the evening
out across the sloughs
singing the spirits song

        The stove needs tending,
         a few branches and dry grass

   The saints go where they will
   though they have no will of their own

"It is not I…"
It is definitely not I
but the eye's light,
a lantern to the body gone out
gone down

Hey papa, please let me pass
see, I bring the sacrifice
every drop, every note
the voices rising and falling
until there is nothing left

1	3	psyche	ψυχή
3	1	pneuma	πνεύμα
0	0	ekstasis	έκσταση

When March comes a third season
and the house is quiet
in the dry wind's roar
and the sun is a burnished gold

When she has become a lion
(and an eagle and a mountain)
and walks on molten glass
across a sea of shattered, useless weaponry
The cities have disappeared
The villagers run to embrace her

In that quiet house

in that third season
she lights a sky blue candle
Doves settle out across the field
and watch the warm light rise

In the dream
I have returned home
I am pruning a pear tree of dead branches
but the branches are full of fruit

She lights a candle
and the night starts singing
Every shadow is released
in radiant joy

> The oblivion of self
> is not
> the self's oblivion

$$3 = 1 = 0$$

nothing but blue
nothing but
nothing
no

> To surrender completely, utterly
> To be broken
> as the earth is broken

as the seed is broken
and surrenders its spirit
so the sky is broken
and the rain pours down

as shadows dim and fade
into the maker of their form

"the freeing of the dust"
the fiery thorn

Prayer.
Faith.
Knowledge.
Death.
Unknowing.
Reality.
Wisdom.
Love.
Heaven.

And heaven is abundantly empty
and breathing glorious mystery
in the body she made

. . . .

Epilogue

How many Easters past was that?
before the slaughtered lamb?
before the apes climbed down from the trees
to kiss the angel of the Word?

We were in an oak paneled room
You were wearing a white cotton dress
I remember the phonograph,
and the slow, close waltz
beneath the paschal moon

I remember your eyes
and the blood stained sheets
wound in the roots of a tree

The crying light
out of such a splendid, shattered night
      How do you explain
      to a child so beautifully conceived
      that even when death finds him
      it cannot hold him?
      Not in the earth
      Not in the water
      Not even the boundless skies
      can contain such passion

The phonograph winds down
The room is stripped bare
and we are alone, naked,

embracing against the cold
waiting
for the moon to break the last day open

Praise for Jake Berry and *Trilogy: Kenosis*

"You must enter the house / without entering it." Jake Berry discovers while inventing miracles in each noticed silence. This brilliantly spiritual poetry changes the listener. The poet tells us "Aristotle uses the word 'psyche' for both soul and butterfly." Then, "Heaven is empty. Everything depends upon it." We share Berry's recognition that "The pilgrimages have taken their toll." In such common ground, the shared body draws from his wisdom. We go forward. "The stove needs tending / a few branches and dry grass." Always work to do the simple and the spiritual, until

> The phonograph winds down
> The room is stripped bare
> and we are alone, naked,
> embracing against the cold
> waiting
> for the moon to break the last day open

—Sheila E. Murphy

Jake Berry is hands-down one of the finest poets writing today. He has an ear for interior sound like few others, and an unshakable faith in poetry as a portal to the luminous. I have never been anything but inspired when I read him. There is fire and ice in his words and great devotion.

—Neeli Cherkovski

Aphorisms of silence: Jake Berry's recent book *Trilogy:Kenosis* (emptying) explores the world of the unspoken in a spare and lyrical eloquence that separates silence from space. Haunting dislocations of the body from the soul, a wandering in the epic sense though a broken post-modern language. Even in the complex longer poems emptiness sounds like a death knell, informed by an archaic mystical sense and yearning, qualities rare in contemporary poetry

> of number there is only
> a chasm
> of every form
> emptying

—Ivan Argüelles

In *Trilogy:Kenosis* Jake Berry empties the Greek psyche of Latin animus to find in the Gothic dark endless images for the soul. Then those images empties of light. Then voids the light, leaving only the poem, the drowned voice shining impossibly through entropy's curse. The word surgeon performs in this operating theater the miracle of nothing. And Jesus, blood dripping from his lips, turns to Arjuna and quotes the last stanzas with, at last, the question to the answer. This blurb is just words. *Trilogy:Kenosis* is something beyond the soul of mineral, the animus of vegetable, the psyche of animal. To read these poems is to drift beyond any and all tongue noise. These poems you feel feel you.

—Willie Smith

How does one bridge the relationship between the divine as one perceives it and one's suffering, desiring, joyful self—oneself in the world? How does rid oneself of the realm of Ego? In Christian theology, kenosis is the concept of the self-emptying of one's own will and becoming entirely receptive to God and the divine will. Saint John of the Cross' classic work, *The Dark Night of the Soul* is an attempt to depict such a process. Kenosis is also the message of the ecstatic concluding lines of Dante's Divina Commedia: *E'n la sua voluntade e nostra pace,* "In his will is our peace."

How does an American, a Southern multitalented poet located in the music-saturated region of Florence, Alabama do it? "If we have been in that house," writes Jake Berry in the opening passage to this work,

> it is no longer a house
>   but a field
>
> charged
> resonant
>
> mound
> & stone
>
> after Beth-el
> a dream like lightning
>
> unkempt in all his ways
>
> These are the vestments
> Triune
> Polyphonic

> a cradle
> made of voices
> a cradle
> before the interruption
> (before the incision)
> of glass

There is nothing in that passage that is not exact—what the French call *le mot juste*. If the passage is nonetheless puzzling and enigmatic it is because it is constantly struggling to get beyond its perfectly conventional syntax into a realm of mystery, to force the words beyond syntax until they arrive at "a cradle / made of voices." Here, syntax is selfhood, and language is a pure reaching beyond, "before the interruption / (before the incision)," into a deliberately other realm. Is this a Christian work invoking a Tri-partite God? I can't tell you, but I can say this: Trilogy: Kenosis is a stretching of language into a realm we both can and cannot comprehend. It is not "one thing." That the passage is beautiful, even breathtaking, goes almost without saying: all you have to do is speak it aloud. Yet its beauty is a function of its essential yearning. It is precisely an emptying out, kenosis. I can't think of anyone else who is doing such work or who is capable of taking such risks: this is a poet who recognizes deep sorrow but who adds, in ecstasy (etymologically "standing outside oneself"), "our sorrow / cannot prevent spring arriving."

—Jack Foley

Death and rebirth are recurring themes. Like all good poetry, the reader's mind is allowed to wonder, grasping those stones that fall within our reach. As I have so often said, there is genius here, palpable and true. It stirs the mind, the soul, the heart and takes us where we desire and where we fear simultaneously.

The words he rolls across my pages challenge me and push me down and force me to fight back. Who am I if I cannot fight back?

Then comes the gem:

> Memory is more
> than what we remember and imagine –
> It is the past made sacred

A truth so deeply profound it pulls us in and stirs our humanity. We are what we consume and what we read is food for the soul.

There is no questioning the religious nature of this work. It is a bearing of the soul and a sort of confession. We cannot be surprised that our hero has found religion in the autumn of his journey. He too needs the comfort of his love in the lonely hours of night. But his is no comfortable acceptance of the lord thy god. His is a struggle and a challenge to the orthodox light. His is a poet's religion. His heaven is empty yet it is a place that welcomes all thinking sentient beings.

Once again Jake Berry has taken me to a place I would not go. Not on my own. Not at this time in my life. But it is a place I need to go. It is a place that gives life meaning even as it eviscerates all understanding. I understand.

> Oblivion is not the opposite of memory.
> It is its companion and completion.

I understand. There is warmth and hope in this lonely place. And we are not alone. We are guided by the poet just as Dante once was.

Like Dante, Jake Berry is a master of words and thought and prayer. In *Trilogy:Kenosis* he has given us a work that demands to be read again and again, even to our dying day.

—Jack Random, Author of *Hard Times: The Wrath of an Angry God*

Jake Berry's poetry defies attempts to categorise it; such is its encompassing reach into a myriad of poetic styles and forms, which it deconstructs and reassembles in ways that are novel and pleasing.

The poems in this collection continue this standard, and express themselves in an assortment of registers, poetic modes and textual arrangements; and comprise elements that are: dreamlike, elliptical, philosophical, theological, koan-like and mythical—along with a measured use of classical and scientific allusion, and textual and numerical "samplings".

But perhaps most importantly, the poems never stray from the one essential element poetry needs to have if it is to appeal to more than solely the intellect—musicality.

—Jeffrey Side

CPSIA information can be obtained
at www.ICGtesting.com
Printed in the USA
FSHW011643041118
53432FS